Abnormal Psychology
The Problem of Maladaptive Behavior

Tenth Edition

Media and Research Update

Irwin G. Sarason
University of Washington

Barbara R. Sarason
University of Washington

UPDATES PROVIDED BY

Sandra Harris
Troy State University of Montgomery

PEARSON
Prentice
Hall

Upper Saddle River, New Jersey 07458

Senior Acquisitions Editor: Jeff Marshall
Editor-in-Chief: Leah Jewell
Editorial Assistant: Jill Liebowitz
Media Project Manager: Jennifer M. Collins
Executive Marketing Manager: Sheryl Adams
Marketing Assistant: Jeanette Laforet
Managing Editor: Joanne Riker
Assistant Managing Editor: Maureen Richardson
Production Editor: Nicole Girrbach
Manufacturing Buyer: Tricia Kenny
Creative Design Director: Leslie Osher
Designer: Kathy Mystkowska
Cover Design: Kathy Mystkowska
Cover Illustration/Photo: Jose Ortega/Stock Illustration Source, Inc.
Manufacturing Manager: Nick Sklitsis
Printer/Binder: Demand Production Center

Pearson Education Ltd.
Pearson Education Australia PTY, Limited
Pearson Education Singapore, Pte. Ltd.
Pearson Education North Asia Ltd.
Pearson Education, Canada, Ltd.
Pearson Educación de Mexico, S.A. de C.V.
Pearson Education–Japan
Pearson Education Malaysia, Pte. Ltd.

10 9 8 7 6 5 4 3 2 1
ISBN 0-13-184267-6

Contents

Videos In Abnormal Psychology

It's one thing to read about abnormal psychology in your text. To get a true understanding, though, it helps to see and hear individuals who are diagnosed with a range of psychological disorders. This CD-ROM gives you an opportunity to do just that, with twenty videos showing interviews with patients, researchers, and clinicians. Each video opens with an introduction and is followed by questions relating it to major concepts in abnormal psychology. Here are the topics and videos you'll find on the CD-ROM.

Diagnosis and Assessment
Administration of Projective Tests:
   Dr. Ruth Munroe

Treatments
Client-Centered Therapy: Dr. Carl Rogers

Anxiety Disorders
Obsessive Compulsive Disorder: The Case of Ed
Panic Disorder: The Case of Jerry

Somatoform, Dissociative, and Factitious Disorders
Dissociative Identity Disorder: The Three
   Faces of Eve
Dissociative Identity Disorder:
   Doctor Holliday Milby

Mood Disorders and Suicide
Bipolar Disorder: The Case of Craig
Depression: The Case of Helen

Personality Disorders
Antisocial Personality Disorder: The Case of Paul

Eating Disorders
Eating Disorders: Nutritionist Alise Thresh
Anorexia: The Case of Tamora
Bulimia: The Case of Ann

Substance Use Disorders
Substance Abuse: Therapist Jean Obert
Substance Abuse: Therapist Louise Roberts

Gender Identity Disorders and Sexual Dysfunction
Gender Identity Disorder: The Case of Denise

Schizophrenia and Other Psychotic Disorders
Schizophrenia: The Case of Georgiana

Delirium, Dementia, Amnestic Disorders and Other Cognitive Disorders
Alzheimer's Disease: The Case
   of Wilburn "John" Johnson

Childhood Disorders
ADHD: Dr. Raun Melmed
Autism: Dr. Kathy Pratt

Violence and Domestic Abuse
Child Sexual Abuse: The Case of Karen

Abnormal Psychology
The Problem of Maladaptive Behavior

Chapter 4, Stress, Coping, and Maladaptive Behavior

Because of the hectic pace of modern society, individuals often find themselves struggling to keep up with the tempo of daily living. For many, the struggle results in a harrowing, rushed, and stressed life-style. Although most find adaptive methods of coping with the stress, for others the stress becomes the foundation for maladaptive patterns of coping, which in turn lead to clinical reactions such as dissociative disorders.

Among the stress-related disorders, the dissociative disorders are thought to have precursors in early stages of life. For instance, in a study of adults diagnosed with dissociative disorder, Pasquini, Liotti, Mazzotti, Fassone, and Picardi (2002) not only discovered a link between early abuse by caregivers, but also found a link between significant losses experienced by mothers (such as death, marital separation, or health or financial problems) during the first two years of the subjects' life. These researchers concluded, "Unresolved losses and traumas in the caregiver's life may exert disorganizing influences on the infant's attachment either through violent parental behaviour or through simply frightened, but not otherwise maltreating, parental behaviour" (p. 111). The findings uphold the hypothesis that traumatic experience in infancy heightens the predisposition for the manifestation of subsequent dissociative disorders.

In another study, West, Adam, Spreng, and Rose (2001) found early attachment disorganization and dissociative symptoms in a group of adolescents. The researchers recruited patients who were admitted to treatment centers after traumatic family events such as unwanted separation, death, divorce, or abuse. The participants were assessed using the following measures. The Adult Attachment Interview (AAI), which is a semistructured interview constructed to obtain information about attachment relationships and other events early in life. The Youth Self-Report (YSR), developed by Thomas Achenbach, which measures "competencies and problems of individuals 11 to 18 years" (p. 629). West et al. (2001) developed a five-item scale from the YSR to measure the presence of dissociative symptoms. The results revealed that for both male and female adolescents, "unresolved and unclassifiable response to attachment-related trauma was related to dissociative symptoms" (p. 697).

In addition, a third study (Simeon, Gruralnik, Schmeidler, Sirof, & Knutelska, 2001) found a link between interpersonal trauma in childhood and depersonalization disorder (a subcategory of dissociative disorders). The researchers studied adult patients who were diagnosed with depersonalization disorder and compared them with a control group of healthy participants who were free of dissociative disorders and any of the other DSM–IV Axis I or II disorders. Both groups completed the Dissociative Experiences Scale (DES), designed by Bernstein and Putnam (1986) to measure dissociation, and the Childhood Trauma Interview, developed by Fink, Bernstein, Handelsman, Foote, and Lovejoy (1995) to evaluate the occurrence of childhood trauma up to age 18. The study found that although the healthy participants experienced the greater degree of separation loss, patients with depersonalization disorder experienced significantly greater emotional abuse. The major finding of this study was that childhood interpersonal trauma as a whole was highly predictive of a diagnosis of depersonalization, dissociation, pathological dissociation, and depersonalization.

Taken together, the results from these studies and others lead to the suggestion that disorganized attachment which occurs early in life predisposes individuals to dissociative pathology later in life. This theory also offers a possible method for understanding the theoretical etiology of the disorder.

On another front, research by Pekala, Angelini, and Kumar (2001) uncovered a link between "fantasy-proneness" and dissociation. These researchers studied patients who were admitted to a VA medical center substance abuse unit to investigate the relationship between dissociation, child abuse, and fantasy-proneness. Dissociation was measured using the DES (Bernstein & Putnam, 1986); fantasy-proneness was measured using the Inventory of Childhood Memories and Imaginings (ICMI) developed by Sanders and Becker-Lausen (1995); and child abuse was measured by the Child Abuse Trauma (CAT) scale developed by Wilson and Barber (1983b) to measure negative experiences and childhood and adolescence. The results indicated that fantasy-proneness was as strong an indicator of dissociation as was child abuse in a population of male substance abusers. The researchers concluded that in attempting to understand the etiology of dissociation, clinicians should consider both fantasy-proneness and child abuse as precursors of the disorder.

References

Bernstein, E.M. & Putnam, F.W. (1986). Development, reliability, and validity of a dissociation scale. *Journal of Nervous Mental Disorders, 174,* 727–735.

Fink, L. A., Bernstein, D., Handelsman, L., Foote, J., & Lovejoy, M. (1995). Initial validity and reliability of the Childhood Trauma Interview: A new multidimensional measure of childhood interpersonal trauma. *American Journal of Psychiatry, 152,* 1329–1335.

Pasquini, P., Liotti, G., Mazzotti, E., Fassone, G., & Picardi, A. (2002). Risk factors in the early family life of patients suffering from dissociative disorders. *Acta Psychiatrica Scandinavia, 105,* 111–116.

Pekala, R. J., Angelini, F., & Kumar, V. K. (2001). The importance of fantasy-proneness in dissociation: A replication. *Contemporary Hypnosis, 18(4),* 204–214.

Sanders, B. & Becker-Lausen, E. (1995). The measurement of psychological maltreatment: Early data on the child abuse and trauma scale. *Child Abuse and Neglect, 19,* 315–323.

Simeon, D., Gruralnik, O., Schmeidler, J., Sirof, B., & Knutelska, M. (2001). The role of childhood interpersonal trauma in depersonalization disorder. *American Journal of Psychiatry, 158(7),* 1027–1033.

West, M., Adam, K., Spreng, S., & Rose, S. (2001). Attachment disorganization and dissociative symptoms in clinically treated adolescents. *Canadian Journal of Psychiatry, 46(7),* 627–631.

Wilson, S. C. & Barber, T. X. (1983b). *The Inventory of Childhood Memories and Imaginings (ICMI).* Framingham, MA: Cushing Hospital.

Chapter 5, Bodily Dysfunction: Eating and Sleeping Problems, and Psychophysiological Disorder

Eating Disorders

Eating disorders are maladaptive behaviors with both physical and psychological consequences (Fairburn & Harrison, 2003). Such disorders are also likely to pose a financial burden because the course of treatment is elaborate and its other associated costs are often quite high (Frost, Murphy, Webster, & Schmidt, 2003). Eating disorders are divided into three categories: anorexia nervosa, bulimia, and atypical disorders. The first two disorders are unified by a common theme: patients, both male and female, tend to place exaggerated emphasis on their size and shape. Anorexia nervosa typically manifests itself during the teenage years, and it is the one eating disorder with a high mortality rate; most deaths result from secondary causes or suicide. Bulimia typically does not occur until later in life. Atypical disorders are those which are not easily classified (Fairburn & Harrison, 2003).

Though found in both sexes, anorexia nervosa is more prevalent in females, and most research has investigated the occurrence of eating disorders in women.

Fewer studies have focused on the disorder as it occurs in males. In fact, one of the diagnostic criteria for anorexia nervosa in females is amenorrhea, or cessation of the menstrual cycle, for at least three consecutive months. While it is clear that this criterion does not apply to males, there has been little talk of deleting or even replacing it for males (Woodside, 2002). In view of the present diagnostic criteria for most eating disorders, one of the current concerns is that the rate of eating disorders among males may be underestimated. One study (Woodside et al., 2000) revealed that the prevalence of eating disorders in men might be close to 25% of the rate for women. For anexoria nervosa, the researchers found that the rate of affliction was about 1 male for every 2 females. The results further revealed that men were more likely than women to experience partial syndrome bulimia nervosa. These researchers also noted that males are less likely to seek treatment for the condition; their reluctance may be in part due to the fact that males may not view themselves as vulnerable to the disorder. With this fact in mind, it is clear that society needs to be better educated about the risks of and hazards associated with eating disorders in males.

In a recent study, Frost et al. (2003) posed this question: "Are top journals biased against eating disorder topics?" These researchers proposed that although eating disorders carry the same physical, social, emotional, and psychological burdens as other types of disorders (specifically, panic disorder and agoraphobia), the condition receives less attention in leading psychiatric, medical, and psychological periodicals and journals. These researchers compared the number of articles published on eating disorders and the number published on panic disorder and/or agoraphobia for a 5-year period from 1996 to 2001. During this period, 169 articles on anorexia nervosa and 365 articles on panic disorder and/or agoraphobia were published, a ratio of almost 1:2. These researchers ruled out the possibility that the publication differences might be due to differences in funding. For the 5-year period, 200 grants were awarded for the study of anorexia nervosa and 280 were awarded for the study of panic disorder and/or agoraphobia; hence, the funding for the two categories of disorders was not reflected in the publication rate. The researchers speculated that the submission rates for papers on the two categories of disorders might be equal, but the difference in rates of publication could be attributable to the fact that fewer articles on anorexia nervosa are accepted for publication. The authors suggested that the difference may reflect a bias against eating disorders in some of the leading psychiatric journals. "The fact that anorexia nervosa and bulimia nervosa are predominantly female disorders compared to the more equal sex distribution of panic disorder and agoraphobia may contribute to the view that eating disorders are of lesser importance" (p. 365). The researchers recommend that editors and publishers monitor more closely the types of articles that are being published so as not to inadvertently discriminate against certain disorders.

Etiology As with most psychological disorders, the specific causes of eating disorders are difficult to determine. In general, clinicians agree that there is some interaction between genetic predispositions and environmental influences (Fairburn & Harrison, 2003). A recent study by Bulik et al. (2003) focused on the relationship between eating disorders and perfectionism. The researchers used a modified version of the Multidimensional Perfectionism Scale (MPS) to measure aspects of perfectionist behaviors and attitudes. The original scale contained several subscales that measured parental and individual characteristics. In this study the researchers used only those items that pertained to individual characteristics. Diagnostic data were also collected and analyzed on the lifetime incidence of psychiatric and substance use disorders of participants. From the items on the MPS, the researchers constructed three subscales: (a) concern over mistakes, (b) doubts about actions, and (c) personal standards. The results indicated that the concern over mistakes subscale evidenced a strong positive association with anorexia nervosa and bulimia nervosa, but the subscale was not associated with the presence of other disorders. The researchers concluded that although an aspect of perfectionism, concern over mistakes, may be associated with eating disorders, it is not necessarily indicative of other psychopathology.

Treatment Without a firm understanding of the etiology of eating disorders, researchers find it difficult to develop effective means of treatment for them. Most research has focused on the treatment of bulimia nervosa; little has been written on effective treatments for anorexia nervosa and the atypical eating disorders. In general, the research findings on effective treatment for bulimia nervosa can be summarized as follows: cognitive-behavior therapy focusing on altering particular types of behavior tends to be the most effective, and the use of antidepressant drugs may be helpful in curbing behaviors associated with bulimia nervosa.

In the absence of guidelines for treating those individuals who do not respond to cognitive-behavior therapy, Fairburn and Harrison (2003) offer the following guidelines for managing the treatment program of patients diagnosed with anorexia nervosa.

1. Assist patients in acknowledging and accepting the need for help, and be proactive in helping patients sustain their motivation to seek treatment.

2. Develop a program that will help the patient gain weight and thus reduce or minimize the impact of malnutrition associated with the disorder.
3. Address patients cognitive interpretation of their shape and weight, their eating habits, and their general psychosocial functioning.
4. Use compulsory treatment where necessary to protect the health and welfare of the individual patient.

Chronic Fatigue Syndrome

Chronic fatigue syndrome (CFS) is a disorder marked by the presence of overwhelming and sustained symptoms of fatigue which lack a medical origin and which persist for longer than 6 months. The prevalence of the disorder in Western societies ranges from 0.007% to 2.8% of the general population (Afari & Buchwald, 2003; Sundbom, Henningsson, Holm, Soderbergh, & Evengard, 2002). In spite of the research that has been conducted, the cause of CFS is largely unknown. In a review of the literature on CFS, Afari and Buchwald (2003) reported on a number of studies that identified several possible causal factors, including genetic inheritance, abnormalities of the central nervous system, malfunctions of the immune system, disruption of sleep, inability to tolerate exercise, presence of other psychiatric disorders, and attributions, perception, and coping style. A recent study (Sundbom et al., 2003) sought to determine whether specific defensive patterns of behavior were related to the presence of CFS. The study included 45 people; 13 were diagnosed with CFS, 19 were diagnosed with conversion disorder, and 13 were healthy control participants. All participants were administered a three-part assessment. A Defense Mechanism Test repeatedly exposed them to anxiety-provoking pictures. Participants then gave verbal reports, and drew pictures of what they saw. An After Reading Scale (ARS) was used to measure a person's ability to interpret one's internal emotional state as it was aroused by patients presented in videotaped interview in various emotional states. A paper-and-pencil questionnaire solicited information about various life events. The results of the study indicated that patients with CFS reported more negative life events and greater difficulty in handling negative affect as it was aroused by the Defense Mechanism Test.

References

Afari, N. & Buchwald, D. (2003). Chronic fatigue syndrome: A review. *American Journal of Psychiatry, 160(2)*, 221–236.

Bulik, C. M., Tozzi, F., Anderson, C., Mazzeo, S. E., Aggen, S., & Sullivan, P. F. (2003). The relationship between eating disorders and components of perfectionism. *American Journal of Psychiatry, 160(2)*, 366–368.

Fairburn, C. G. & Harrison, J. (2003). Eating disorders. *Lancet, 361*, 407–416.

Frost, S., Murphy, R., Webster, P., & Schmidt, U. (2003). Are top journals biased against eating disorders? *American Journal of Psychiatry, 160(2)*, 363–366.

Sundbom, E., Henningsson, M., Holm, U., Soderbergh, S., & Evengard, B. (2002). Possible influence of defenses and negative life events on patients with chronic fatigue syndrome: A pilot study. *Psychological Reports, 91(3)*, 963–988.

Woodside, D. B. (2002). Eating disorders in men: An overview. *Healthy Weight Journal, 16(4)*, 52–55.

Woodside, D. B., Garfinkel, F. E., Lin, E., Goering, P., Kaplan, A.S., & Goldbloom, D.S. (2000). Men with full and partial syndrome eating disorders: Community comparisons with non-eating disordered men and eating disordered women. *American Journal of Psychiatry, 158*, 570–574.

Chapter 6, Disorders of Bodily Preoccupation

Somatoform Disorders

Recent research (Bass & May, 2002) has focused on a particular subcategory of somatoform disorders, chronic multiple functional somatic (CMFS) symptoms. Individuals with this disorder "typically have a long-standing pattern of presenting with various functional symptoms, have had multiple referrals for investigation of these, and are regarded by their doctors as difficult to help" (p. 323). It is estimated that 4% of the overall population will experience CMFS. One of the major dangers associated with the condition is overdiagnosis of somatic disorders and the subsequent overprescribing of medication to treat the symptoms. Most patients are women, and the condition is often associated with some form of childhood trauma such as emotional deprivation or physical and sexual abuse. Because such patients tend to seek out more than one doctor for treatment of their symptoms, assessment and management of the disorder becomes problematic. A physician may not be aware that the patient is or has been seeking treatment elsewhere. Unless the patient has a primary care physician who maintains the appropriate records, diagnosis of the disorder becomes an elusive endeavor. Although CMFS is relatively uncommon, encounters with such patients

are often of such a nature as to not be forgotten. Because of the elusiveness of the various symptoms, both the doctor and patient often feel frustrated by the treatment process. To effectively manage patients, doctors must be aware of the interpersonal difficulties associated with the disorder, and doctors must be ever vigilant in protecting the patient from the harm associated with over-diagnosis and overprescribing of medication. When appropriate, general medical doctors should refer the patient for psychiatric services.

Reference

Bass, C. & May, S. (2002). Chronic multiple functional somatic symptoms. *British Medical Journal, 325(7359)*, 323–326.

Chapter 7, Anxiety Disorders

This group is one of the two most commonly occurring psychiatric disorders in the United States; mood disorders are the other (Valente, 2002). A recent study by Hettema, Neale, and Kendler (2001) found a genetic predisposition for a range of anxiety disorders. In a meta-analytic study of the disorders, these researchers found a significant correlation between the prevalence of panic disorder, generalized anxiety disorder, phobias, and obsessive-compulsive disorder among first-degree relatives. Cumulatively, the meta-analytic study yielded estimated heritability indices of 30% to 40% across the spectrum of anxiety disorders. Although environmental factors undoubtedly influence the occurrence of anxiety disorders, the findings of this study led the researchers to conclude that a large source of risk comes from familial genetics.

Obsessive-Compulsive Disorder (OCD)

Among the family of anxiety disorders, a great deal of research has been conducted on OCD. The disorder occurs twice as often as others such as panic disorder and schizophrenia, and unlike other disorders, the rate of occurrence for males and females is roughly the same at 47% and 53%, respectively (Valente, 2002). Much of past research focused on the occurrence of the disorder in adults; however, OCD is common in children. The Harvard Mental Health Letter (2002a) reported that 1% to 3% of U.S. children are affected by the disorder, with the age of onset as early as 3 years, and that childhood OCD is more common in males than in females.

A recent study focused on a spectrum of childhood traits that might indicate obsessive personality in adult women. Anderluh, Tchanturia, Rabe-Hesketh, and

Treasure (2003) compared a group of female patients diagnosed with eating disorders and a group of healthy participants to determine the correlation between childhood personality traits, particularly those that reflect obsessive-compulsive behavior, and the development of eating disorders in adults. The data collection consisted of an interview and administration of the self-report Maudsley Obsessive-Compulsive Inventory, a 30-item instrument that measures the four obsessive complaints of checking, washing, doubting, and slowness. The results indicated that adult OCD is significantly related to childhood behaviors that could be considered obsessive-compulsive in nature, thus supporting previous findings that suggest a comorbidity between OCD and eating disorders.

As with most disorders, there is continuing discussion regarding the degree to which nature, or biology, predisposes individuals to developing OCD and the degree to which the environment influences its onset. Past data suggested that the vulnerability for risk of OCD is 9% for individuals with a close family member diagnosed with OCD and 2% for the general population. The heritability index of OCD for identical twins can be as high as 68% (Harvard Mental Health Letter, 2002a). A number of studies have investigated the neurobiological basis of OCD. Tot, Özge, Çömelekoglu, Yazici, and Bal (2002) detected decreased electrical activity in the brains of patients diagnosed with OCD. Using a qualitative electroencephalographic (QEEG) technique, the researchers compared characteristics of 22 right-handed patients with OCD to a comparison group of 20 healthy, right-handed participants. None of the patients had taken any drugs that would affect the central nervous system (CNS) in the 2 weeks prior to the study. No members of the control group had any history of psychiatric disorders, and none had ever taken drugs that would affect their CNS. "Each subject was seated in a soundproof, light-controlled, well-ventilated recording room while 30 minutes of eyes-closed resting EEG data were collected" (p. 540). Upon analyzing the data, the researchers discovered a dysfunction in the frontotemporal region of the brains of patients with OCD as compared to the control participants. In particular, the data revealed decreased activity in the delta, and to some extent theta, wave patterns of patients with OCD.

Post Traumatic Stress Disorder (PTSD)

As the number of traumatic events in our society increases, the number of people who experience the trauma will also increase. Consequently, the number of individuals at risk for post-traumatic stress disorder (PTSD) will continue to rise. Originally observed in U.S. Vietnam-era veterans (Harvard Mental Health Letter, 2001), PTSD is the consequence of a person's exposure to a traumatic event. The disorder does not carry with it a specified timeline; however, in most cases the symptoms appear within 3 months of the occurrence of the event. The disorder generally carries with it three sets of symptoms: (1) re-experiencing the event in the form of flashbacks, dreams, and recurring mental images; (2) avoidance symptoms such as disavowing feelings, avoiding places and activities associated with the event, or social withdrawal from friends and family; and (3) elevated arousal of the autonomic nervous system as evidenced by heightened startle response, hypervigilance, and irritability (Feinstein & Owen, 2002; Purves & Erwin, 2002).

Etiology Although the exact etiology of PTSD is not known, there is research indicating that some individuals may be genetically predisposed to manifesting symptoms of the disorder after experiencing a traumatic event (Stein, 2002). Several studies have indicated that people experiencing PTSD tend to have a smaller hippocampus (an inner brain structure) than healthy control participants. Villareal et al. (2002) found that decreased concentrations of the chemical N-acetylaspartate (NAA) in the hippocampus were correlated with PTSD. This study compared a group of civilian participants with PTSD to a control group. After obtaining MRIs of the brains for both groups, the researchers discovered that the group with PTSD evidenced reduced NAA, which is associated with reduced neuronal integrity in the hippocampus.

It is accepted that PTSD is triggered by environmental events. Most individuals who undergo a traumatic experience will have some form of emotional reaction to the event; however, not all will experience PTSD (Stein, 2002). The question then becomes "What aspect of the stressful event predisposes some individuals to PTSD and not others?" One study (Harvard Mental Health Letter, 2002b) found evidence suggesting that what happens after the stressful event affects whether an individual experiences PTSD. Those individuals who experienced stressful life events after the trauma were more predisposed to PTSD; however, stressful life events before the traumatic experience had little effect on the manifestation of PTSD. A second study revealed that those individuals who had experienced several kinds of trauma were more predisposed to manifesting PTSD. In this study, PTSD was most common in those who had experienced personal trauma. The data from these studies illuminate the complexity in attempting to understand the etiological bases for PTSD.

Although the exact cause of PTSD is unknown, the data indicate that certain populations are more prone to the disorder than others. In particular, women and those whose jobs place them in the position of having to deal with the aftermath of a traumatic event are most vulnerable. A number of studies (Breslau, 2002; Purves & Erwin, 2002; Stein, 2002) have indicated that women are far more likely to experience PTSD than men. It is widely accepted that rates of PTSD are high among members of certain occupations, such as military combat or peacekeeping operations (Gabriel & Neal, 2002), and among professional caregivers such as doctors, emergency personnel, and social workers (Feinberg, 2002), but the effects of traumatic events on people in other occupations have not been as well studied. Feinstein and Owen (2002) reported the effects of traumatic stress in a comparison study that revealed that war journalists, especially photographers, experienced significantly more emotional reactions such as PTSD, depression, and psychological distress than their domestic counterparts. The photographers also experienced more occurrences of physical illness than did their print-based counterparts, and the emotional difficulties suffered by the photographers, for the most part, went unnoticed.

Feinberg (2002) proposed that teachers and school administrators are also subject to vicarious traumatization—a form of burnout that is often experienced by trained professional caregivers. Feinberg proposed that the effects of burnout are even more severe because educators are not trained as caregivers. He argued that educators must be cognizant of the fact that, even though they may not have experienced trauma directly, they are susceptible to burnout as they attempt to fulfill their professional roles; one of those roles involves comforting and encouraging children in the aftermath of traumatic events.

Prevalence According to Helzer, Robins, and McEvoy (as cited in Purves & Erwin, 2002), the first epidemiological study of PTSD symptomology, which was conducted in 1987, reported lifetime rates (percentage of adults who experience symptoms) of PTSD in the United States of 0.5% for males and 1.3% for females. In a 1991 study of young adults in the United States, Breslau, Davies, Andreski, and Peterson (as cited in Purves & Erwin, 2002) found that 39.1% of participants had experienced a traumatic event, and 23.6% of that group developed symptoms of PTSD. This study found a lifetime prevalence rate of PTSD of 9.2%.

Purves and Erwin (2002) investigated the prevalence of PTSD among British students from a single university. Participants were given a questionnaire that was developed by the researchers to measure the presence, frequency, and recency of PTSD symptoms. Of the participants, 39% reported having experienced a traumatic event. The respondents indicated that they ranged in age from their mid to late teens at the time of occur-

rence. The average length of elapsed time since the event was 7.2 years. The results indicated that 23.3% of the sample were either currently classified or had been in the past classified as having symptoms of PTSD. The results also revealed that females experienced a significantly higher rate of clinical PTSD than their male counterparts; the rates were 26.1% and 17.2%, respectively. The findings of this study were consistent with those of Breslau et al.

Purves and Erwin (2002) indicated that participants in their study had been exposed to traumatic events in their teens, leading to the question, "What is the prevalence of PTSD-related symptoms in children and adolescents?" According to Yule (2001) there is not a widely accepted theory about PTSD in children. However, in the aftermath of a traumatic event, children manifest a host of symptoms that parallel PTSD symptoms found in adults, including (a) repetitive, intrusive thoughts that begin almost immediately after a traumatic event; (b) flashbacks that result in the child re-experiencing the event; (c) sleep disturbances such as bad dreams, nightmares, and waking through the night, especially in the first few weeks after the traumatic event; (d) fear of the dark; (e) separation anxiety from parents; (f) irritable or angry moods; (g) pressure to talk about the event; (h) difficulty discussing the event with parents or friends; (i) cognitive changes such as poor concentration and memory problems; and (j) hypervigilance to possible danger in the environment. A recent study by Yule (as cited in Yule, 2001) investigated the prevalence of PTSD among children who had experienced traffic accidents. The data revealed that 25% to 30% of the children developed symptoms of PTSD. In a study by Yule, Bolton, and Udwin, et al. (as cited in Yule, 2001), 52% of 400 adolescents who survived the sinking of a cruise ship in 1988 developed symptoms of PTSD in the initial weeks after the accident, and 34% met the criteria for symptoms 5 to 8 years after the sinking. The youths also developed a host of other psychiatric disorders, which remained highest for those who manifested PTSD.

Probably one of the greatest obstacles to diagnosing PTSD in children may be the methods of assessment that are used. Quite often methods used for adults are developmentally inappropriate for children (Yule, 2001). Hence, it is necessary that some form of assessment be established which is appropriate for assessing symptoms of PTSD in children. Recently, Foa, Johnson, Feeny, and Treadwell (2001) developed the Child PTSD Symptom Scale (CPSS), a self-report instrument designed to measure PTSD severity in traumatized children and adolescents. The CPSS was modeled after the Posttraumatic Diagnostic Scale developed by Foa, Cashman, Jaycox, and Perry (1997) to measure PTSD in adults. The language was changed to reflect developmentally appropriate vocabulary that would help children understand the items. The CPSS contains 17 items that reflect the diagnostic criteria for PTSD symptoms as presented in the DSM–IV. The CPSS instrument yields three scores: re-experiencing, avoidance, and arousal. These researchers studied children who had survived an earthquake in California. "The results suggest that the CPSS is a useful tool for the assessment of post-traumatic stress disorder (PTSD) severity and for the screening of PTSD diagnosis among traumatized children" (Foa et al., 2001, p. 376).

Treatment A range of options are available for treating symptoms of PTSD. Livanou (2001) wrote a review article of the various psychological treatments for PTSD. Among those treatments, cognitive-behavior therapy (CBT) holds special promise. A particular subcategory of CBT, exposure therapy, involves "repeated and prolonged confrontation with anxiety evoking objects or situations, until anxiety is gradually reduced" (p. 181). Recently, Rothbaum and Schwartz (2002) did a review of relevant research findings on the efficacy of CBT, specifically, exposure therapy, for treating symptoms of PTSD. Five out of six studies found that exposure therapy had positive effects on symptoms associated with PTSD. Two studies found that exposure therapy was effective in treating PTSD symptoms in sexual-assault survivors. Another study found that exposure therapy was effective for treating survivors of a variety of traumas. Collectively, the studies evaluated by Livanou demonstrate the efficacy of exposure therapy for treating PTSD. Subsequent to this literature review, Rothbaum and Schwartz (2002) summarized the following guidelines for treating PTSD: (a) patients should remain in treatment until the symptoms decrease; (b) patients should be allowed to progress at their own pace; (c) patients should be encouraged to reveal as much detail about the traumatic event as possible, especially the parts they considered to be the worst; and (d) therapists must gauge their response to patients because problematic responses from the therapist frequently impede the progress of the patient.

References

Anderluh, M. J., Tchanturia, K., Rabe-Hesketh, S., & Treasure, J. (2003). Childhood obsessive-compulsive personality traits in adult women with eating disorders: Defining a broader eating disorder phenotype. *American Journal of Psychiatry, 160(2),* 242–247.

Breslau, N. (2002) Epidemiologic studies of trauma, posttraumatic stress disorder, and other psychiatric disorders. *Canadian Journal of Psychiatry, 47(10),* 923–929.

Corbett, A. (2002). Some brains more vulnerable to war trauma. *Science Now,* 1–2.

Feinberg, T. (2002). Caring for our caregivers after 9/11. *Education Digest, 67(9),* 8–11.

Feinstein, A. & Owen, J. (2002). War photographers and stress. *Columbia Journalism Review, 41(2),* 51.

Foa, E. B., Cashman, L., Jaycox, L., & Perry, K. (1997). The validation of a self-report measure of posttraumatic stress disorder: The Posttraumatic Diagnostic Scale. *Psychological Assessment, 9,* 445–451.

Foa, E. B., Johnson, K. M., Feeny, N. C., & Treadwell, K. R. H. (2001). The Child PTSD Symptom Scale: A preliminary examination of its psychometric properties. *Journal of Clinical Child Psychology, 30(3),* 376–384.

Gabriel, R. & Neal, L.A. (2002). Post-traumatic stress disorder following military combat or peace keeping. *British Medical Journal, 324(7333),* 340–341.

Harvard Mental Health Letter. (2001, November). Post-traumatic stress disorder. *27(1),* 4–5.

Harvard Mental Health Letter. (2002a, July). Obsessions and compulsions in children. *19(4),* 4–7.

Harvard Mental Health Letter. (2002b, October). What causes post-traumatic stress disorder: Two views. *19(4),* 8.

Hettema, J. M., Neale, M. C., & Kendler, K. S. (2001). A review of meta-analysis of the genetic epidemiology of anxiety disorders. *American Journal of Psychiatry, 158(10),* 1568–1578.

Livanou, M. (2001). Psychological treatments for post-traumatic stress disorder: An overview. *International Review Journal of Psychiatry, 13,* 181–188.

Purves, D. G. & Erwin, P. G. (2002). A study of post-traumatic stress in a student population. *Journal of Genetic Psychology, 163(1),* 89–96.

Rothbaum, B. O. & Schwartz, A. C. (2002). Exposure therapy for posttraumatic stress disorder. *American Journal of Psychotherapy, 56(1),* 59–76.

Stein, M. (2002). Taking aim at posttraumatic stress disorder: Understanding its nature and shooting down myths. *Canadian Journal of Psychiatry, 47(10),* 921–922.

Tot, S., Özge, A., Çömelekoglu, Ü., Yazici, K., & Bal, N. (2002). Association of QEEG findings with clinical characteristics of OCD: Evidence of left frontotemporal dysfunction. *Canadian Journal of Psychiatry, 47(6),* 538–545.

Valente, S. (2002). Obsessive-compulsive disorder. *Perspectives in Psychiatric Care, 38(4),* 125–146.

Villareal, G., Petropopoulous, H., Hamilton, D. A., Rowland, L. M., Horan, W. P., Griego, J. A., et al. (2002). Proton magnetic resonance spectroscopy of the hippocampus and occipital white matter in

PTSD: Preliminary results. *Canadian Journal of Psychiatry, 47(7)*, 666–670.

Yule, W. (2001). Post-traumatic stress disorder in children and adolescents. *International Review of Psychiatry, 13*, 194–200.

Chapter 9, Personality Disorders

Personality disorders are marked by long-term patterns of inappropriate or maladaptive behavior and traits which appear to persist over time (Shea et al., 2002). Hence, it is believed that these disorders do not change much with time. However, research by Seivewright, Tyrer, and Johnson (2002) indicated otherwise. In a 12-year longitudinal study of patients who had "a defined Diagnostic and Statistical Manual (DSM) III disorder, neuroticism, dysthmia, panic disorder, or generalized anxiety disorder" (p. 359), the researchers found that individuals with diagnoses such as antisocial or histrionic personality disorder experienced less severe symptoms over time, and individuals with diagnoses such as schizoid, schizotypal, paranoid, anxious, and fearful personality disorders experienced more severe symptoms over time. Results from this study failed to support the theory that personality characteristics remain stable over time.

The following paragraphs discuss current research on personality disorders in the areas of etiology, diagnosis, long-term effects, and possible treatment.

Etiology

One preliminary view holds that some individuals are biologically susceptible to a range of disorders, especially those that fall along the schizophrenic spectrum. Recently, researchers found a correlation between the size of a particular area of the brain called the caudate nucleus and the presence of schizotypal personality disorder (Levitt et al., 2002). In this study, the researchers compared neuroleptic-naïve male patients with a control group of healthy male patients. Magnetic resonance imaging (MRI) was used to obtain pictures of the brains of all subjects. The data revealed that patients diagnosed with schizotypal personality disorder had significantly smaller volumes in the left and right caudate nucleus than participants in the normal comparison group.

A number of researchers have also investigated the link between various environmental conditions and the later manifestation of psychiatric disorders. One such study conducted by Koponen et al. (2002) revealed a connection between traumatic brain injury (TBI) and psychiatric disorders. The researchers followed a group of individuals who had been referred for neurological evaluation consequent to TBI for a period of up to 30 years. The data revealed a high rate of personality disorders as defined by Axis I and Axis II criteria specified in the DSM–IV. "These findings suggest that traumatic brain injury not only temporarily disturbs brain function but may cause decades-long or even permanent vulnerability to psychiatric disorders in some individuals" (p. 1318). The findings also showed a high rate of major depression among individuals with TBI. Consequently, Kopenen et al. (2002) suggest that individuals who experience TBI should also receive initial and follow-up evaluation for the presence of psychiatric disorders.

Assessment Disordered thinking is prevalent in personality disorders such as schizophrenia, mania, depression, obsessive-compulsive disorder, and a host of others. Effective treatment of such disorders begins with a clinician's ability to diagnose their presence through various methods of assessment. Waring, Neufeld, and Schaefer (2003) described the development and validation of one such measure, the Thought Disorder Questionnaire (TDQ), which is designed to "measure the quantity and quality of disordered thinking in patients with mental disorders" (p. 45). The authors hope that the instrument will help clinicians ascertain the early symptoms of several mental disorders and subsequently predict their course and treatment outcome. The TDQ, a 60-item self-report questionnaire that measures disordered thinking, contains six scales of 10 items each. The reliability estimates for the scales are as follows: content ($r = .78$), control ($r = .83$), orientation ($r = .73$), perception ($r = .76$), fantasy ($r = .81$), and symptoms ($r = .81$). Although the inventory has several limitations (for instance, participants must have reading skills and the ability to complete the form), the developers propose the following clinical implications for the questionnaire: (a) it may be helpful in identifying subjects at high risk for psychosis; (b) results could be applied to follow the progression and treatment outcome of psychological disorders; and (c) results could be used to determine the efficacy of treatment.

In another study, Lenzenweger and Maher (2002) reported data on a new line-drawing task that has possible implications for assessing the likelihood of a person developing schizophrenia. These researchers assessed the relationship between motor performance and psychometric measures of schizotypy, a subcategory of schizophrenia, in a population of college students without a history of psychosis. Participants were asked to draw a square using both their right and left hands. These researchers found that poor performance on the line-drawing task was correlated with four indices of schizotypy as indicated by four psychometric measures of the disorder. Statistical analysis of the results indicated that line-drawing errors were highly correlated with scores of schizotypy as measured by the following instruments: (a) the Perception Aberration Scale (PAS), a 35-item true/false inventory developed by Chapman, Chapman, and Raulin (1978) to measure perceptions of body image and perceptual disturbances; (b) the Magical Ideation Scale (MIS) developed by Eckblad and Chapman (1983) to measure individual beliefs of causation; and (c) the Referential Thinking Scale (REF), developed by Lenzenweger, Bennett, and Lilenfeld (1997) as a "measure of schizotypic referential thinking that assesses both simple and guilty ideas of reference" (p. 546), and the Rosen Paranoid Schizophrenia Scale (PZ. Rosen, 1962) that was developed as an aid in the identification of individuals with paranoid schizophrenia. The results further indicated that when other factors such as intellectual functioning, mental state, and attention levels were controlled for, the line-drawing task remained statistically correlated with higher levels of measured schizotypy as indicated by the PAS and Rosen PZ. The researchers concluded that the line-drawing task might be useful for determining the likelihood of the occurence of schizotypy in other populations.

Borderline Personality Disorder (BPD)

Long-Term Prognosis   Once a client has been diagnosed as having a psychiatric condition, the patient or significant others in the patient's life will seek information regarding the probable long-term outcome of the diagnosis. Recently, Zanarini, Frankenburg, Hennen, and Silk (2003) investigated the long-term prognosis of patients with borderline personality disorder (BPD). In order to investigate the rate of remission for BPD over the course of time, these researchers followed a group of patients who were hospitalized for BPD. The participants were evaluated at the 2-, 4-, and 6-year marks after dismissal from the hospital. At the 2-year point, about 50% of the patients were in remission; the 4-year mark found about 66% in remission; and at the 6-year mark, about 75% of the participants were in remission. In addition, only about 6% of the participants in remission experienced recurrences in the period after follow-up. Results of this study suggest that the overall expectancy for improvement in the symptoms of BPD steadily rises in the years following diagnosis and proper treatment.

Treatment   A panel of experts called the Work Group on Borderline Personality, appointed by the American Psychiatric Association (2001) issued new guidelines for treating BPD. The group recommends psychotherapy combined with psychiatric management, primarily using dialectical behavior therapy and psychodynamic therapy emphasising interpretation to help patients recognize unacknowledged drives and motives that influence their behavior. In regard to using interpretation, the Work Group cautions therapists on the relationship with the client, especially noting the dynamics associated with transference. This phenomenon results in an intense feeling of attachment between the therapist and client which could, if not handled properly, interfere with the therapeutic relationship. In addition, therapists are encouraged to use techniques such as confrontation and clarification. Confrontation refocuses clients on issues that they have been sidestepping or avoiding, and clarification helps clients understand their thoughts and emotions. The use of supportive therapy is also encouraged. In dialectical behavior therapy, the primary focus is on distorted thoughts.

Antisocial Personality Disorder (APD)

Loeber, Burke, and Lahey (2002) investigated the link between childhood psychopathology and antisocial personality disorder (APD). They stated that "clarification of the long-term antecedents and causes of APD is a first step towards specification of preventative interventions" (p. 24). These researchers proposed that because the DSM–IV definition of APD requires that the diagnosis be accompanied by a diagnosis of conduct disorder (CD) in childhood, many of the relevant symptoms of APD may first manifest themselves in other forms of childhood psychopathology such as callous or unemotional behavior, oppositional defiant disorder (ODD), attention-deficit/hyperactivity disorder (ADHD), overanxious disorder (OAD), separation anxiety disorder (SAD), dysthymia, and major depression. They further proposed that longitudinal studies be conducted to investigate the possibility that other forms of childhood psychology may be precursors of APD. Using a modified definition of APD, which excluded CD as a necessary precursor, Loeber, Burke, and Lahey sought to investigate the possible connection between CD and APD.

The study included a group of clinic-referred males who ranged in age from 7 to 12 years at the outset of the study. The boys were followed annually with parent and child interviews until each reached age 17. At ages 18 and 19 the boys were evaluated again, but the parental interviews were no longer conducted. Substance abuse of tobacco, alcohol, marijuana, and other drugs was measured through self-report items. A child behavior checklist was also used to identify various forms of callous or unemotional behavior. Adult criminality was determined by reviewing charges that were based on state and federal agency guidelines. Results indicated that at the developmental stage of adolescence, 59% of the participants met the criteria for the modified definition of APD, and at adulthood (18 or 19 years), 38% met the criteria for APD. Consequently, the presence of CD in childhood was a strong predictor of APD in adolescence, which in turn was a strong predictor of APD in young adulthood. Almost 52% of the participants with CD in adolescence met the criteria for modified APD. The results further indicated that callous or unemotional behavior and drug use independently contributed to the prediction of APD. In summary, those individuals with CD and with additional high scores in the areas of substance abuse (marijuana in particular) and depression were at greatest risk for meeting the criteria for modified APD. Such individuals also tended to evidence higher levels of violent crime.

References

Chapman, L. J., Chapman, J. P., & Raulin, M. L. (1978). Body-image aberration in schizophrenia. *Journal of Abnormal Psychology, 39,* 399–407.

Eckblad, M. & Chapman, L. J. (1983). Magical ideation as an indicator of schizotypy. *Journal of Consulting and Clinical Psychology, 51,* 215–225.

Koponen, S., Taiminen, T., Raija, P., Himanen, L., Isoniemi, H., Heinonen, H., et al. (2002). Axis I and II psychiatric disorders after traumatic brain injury: A 30-year follow-up study. *American Journal of Psychiatry, 159(8),* 1315–1321.

Lenzenweger, M. F., Bennett, M. E., & Lilenfeld, L. R. (1997). The Referential Thinking Scale as a measure of schizotypy: Scale development and initial construct validation. *Psychological Assessment, 9,* 452–463.

Lenzenweger, M. F. & Maher, B. A. (2002). Psychometric schizotypy and motor performance. *Journal of Abnormal Psychology, 111(4),* 546–555.

Levitt, J. J., McCarley, R. W., Dickey, C. C., Voglmaier, M. M., Niznikiewicz, M. A., Seidman, L.J., et al. (2002). MRI study of caudate nucleus volume and its cognitive correlates with neuroepileptic-naïve patients with schizotypal personality disorder. *American Journal of Psychiatry, 159(7),* 1190-1197.

Loeber, R., Burke, J.D., & Lahey, B. F. (2002). What are adolescent antecedents to antisocial personality disorder? *Criminal Behaviour and Mental Health, 12,* 24–36.

Rosen, A. (1962). Development of the MMPI scales based on a reference group of psychiatric patients. *Psychological Monographs, 76* (8, Whole No. 527).

Seivewright, H., Tyrer, P., & Johnson, T. (2002). Change in personality status in neurotic disorders.

Lancet, 359, 2253–2254.

Shea, M. T., Stout, R., Gunderson, J., Morey, L.C., Grilo, C.M., McGlashan, T., Skudol, A.E., et al. (2002). Short-term diagnostic stability of schizotypal, borderline, avoidant, and obsessive-compulsive personality disorders. *American Journal of Psychiatry, 159(12),* 2036–2041.

Waring, E. M., Neufeld, R. W. J., & Schaefer, B. (2003). The Thought Disorder Questionnaire. *Canadian Journal of Psychiatry, 48(1),* 45–51.

Zanarini, M. C., Frankenburg, F. R., Hennen, J., & Silk, K. R. (2003). The longitudinal course of borderline personality psychopathology: 6-year prospective follow-up of the phenomenology of borderline personality disorder. *American Journal of Psychiatry, 160(2),* 274–283.

Chapter 10, Mood Disorders

Mood disorders are one of the two leading psychiatric conditions in the United States. As such, these disorders have become a major challenge in the medical, clinical, and academic professions (Grof, 2002). Because of variability in age related aspects of mood disorders, much past research focused on their occurrence in adults. However, Thorpe, Whitney, Kutcher, and Kennedy (2001) reported differences in the epidemiology, clinical presentation, and treatment options for children, adolescents, and the elderly.

Children and Adolescents

Prevalence The rate of occurrence of depression in U.S. children ranges from 0.4% to 2.5%. This estimate increases to 5% to 10% in adolescence and early adulthood. Although depression is equally likely to occur in males and females in childhood, it is twice as frequent in females compared to males in adolescence and early adulthood (Thorpe et al., 2001). Research and clinical work in the area of childhood mood disorders has been inhibited by several factors (Volkmar, 2002). First, it was thought that such disorders were not common in children. Second, there are compounding factors such as difficulties in making an accurate diagnosis of mood disorders in children. Quite often the initial symptoms of mood disorders may mimic other disorders found in children, such as inattention. Third, there are possible interactions between the disruptions in development caused by the disorder and the degree to which the child's development affects the presenting symptoms of the disorder.

Outcome Children who show symptoms of mood disorders are at a greater risk of manifesting these or other disorders later in life. For instance, children who experience a major depressive episode (MDE) are 90% more likely to manifest MDE in adolescence. In addition, children and adolescents with depressive symptoms are likely to experience other disorders such as anxiety, behavior disorders, and instances of substance abuse. Adolescents who experience depression face a 70% likelihood of experiencing another MDE within 5 years. In addition, there is a strong correlation between childhood MDE and bipolar disorder. Children who experience MDE face a 20% to 40% likelihood of developing bipolar disorder within 5 years of the onset (Thorpe et al., 2001).

Treatment To improve the long-term prognosis of mood disorders in children adolescents, it is imperative that effective diagnostic and treatment programs be implemented so as to minimize the potential social, emotional, and psychosocial burdens caused by the disorders. According to Thorpe et al., (2001), while there are insufficient data to recommend treatment guidelines for preadolescent children, cognitive-behavior therapy (CBT), interpersonal therapy (IPT), pharmacotherapy, and electroconvulsive therapy (ECT) offer effective treatment strategies for adolescents. For ages 8–19 years, CBT has been shown to be effective in treating 59% of cases and IPT has been shown to have response rates of 82%. As for the use of drugs to treat mood disorders in children, Thorpe et al. (2001) recommend that drugs be combined with other forms of treatment such as education as well as individual and family counseling. Several researchers have investigated the effectiveness of various families of drugs to treat mood disorders in children. According to Joffe (2003), selective serotonin reuptake inhibitors (SSRIs) tend to produce greater response rates than the traditional drugs of choice, tricyclic antidepressants (TCAs). Thorpe and colleagues concluded that there is not yet enough information to set forth informed guidelines regarding the use of ECT with children. However, they concluded that the efficacy of treatment and the possible side effects of ECT in adolescents are similar to that found in adults. They warn however, that ECT should only be used as a last resort when the depressive symptoms do not respond to other treatment or when the patient is at imminent risk of harm to self in the form of suicide or bodily mutilations.

The Elderly

Prevalence It is a common belief that mood disorders, especially depression, are a common occurrence among the aging population. However, this may not be the case. Several studies conducted in Canada and the United States have indicated that the lifetime occurrence rate of major depressive disorder (MDD) in adults

65 years and older ranges from 0.4% to 1.45%. In contrast, the rate is 1.4% to 4.8% for men and women, respectively, for the 18–44 age group. However individuals in institutionalized care may be at a higher risk for MDD than their noninstitutionalized counterparts (Thorpe et al., 2001).

Treatment Several researchers have conducted meta-analytic studies of various treatment approaches for depression in older adults. One study by Karel and Hinrichsen (as cited in Thorpe et al., 2001) found that cognitive-behavioral therapy (CBT) and psychodynamic treatment strategies produced better response rates than placebo treatment in SSRI and TCA drug treatment studies. Another study by McCusker, Keller, and Bellavance (as cited in Thorpe et al., 2001) indicated that cognitive treatments such as CBT were superior to no treatment, but treatments that address emotions, such as psychodynamic therapy, were not. Much of the current research has focused on studies in younger patients who are generally in better health. However, a few studies have focused on drug treatment in older adults. According to Thorpe et al. (2001), traditional antidepressant medications are effective in adults, and newer drugs such as TCAs and SSRIs are also effective. However, drug treatment in older patients is correlated with side effects such as constipation, urinary retention, vision problems, and cognitive impairment. Consequently, the choice of drugs for treatment in older adults is likely to depend on their side effects. The use of drugs to treat depression in older adults needs to be closely monitored in order to avoid undesirable side effects.

With regard to ECT in treating MDD in adults, Thorpe et al. (2001) reach this conclusion:

> ECT is still considered safe, rapidly effective, and a well-tolerated treatment for MDD. It has been shown to have good outcomes, even in the presence of significant comorbid conditions, and it is used frequently in the elderly with depression, who are less able to tolerate prolonged response times to pharmacotherapy. Good ECT practice in the elderly requires more careful preanesthetic medical consultation and management, minimization of concomitant pharmacotherapy that may adversely affect cognition, and careful inter- and post-ECT cardiac monitoring. (p. 68)

Traumatic Brain Injury (TBI)

The link between traumatic brain injury (TBI) and mood disorders has been investigated for years. According to Ricardo and Robinson (2002), the estimated prevalence of mood and anxiety disorders among TBI patients ranges from 6% to 77%. However, these researchers contend that few studies have focused on the connection between TBI, mood disorders, and outcome variables. These researchers looked at 155 patients admitted to two different hospitals in the United States for TBI; 66 were admitted to a shock trauma center in Maryland and 89 were admitted to a hospital in Iowa. The patients in these studies were evaluated for a period of 1 to 2 years after the initial injury. These studies produced several important results. First, about 50% of patients with TBI experienced some form of mood disorder during the first year after an injury. The duration ranged from 1.5 months to 1 year, with a mean of 4.7 months. In addition, about 77% of the TBI patients in the second study who experienced MDD also developed symptoms associated with anxiety disorders as compared to 22% of the patients who did not develop mood disorders. The study further revealed that those TBI patients who had a past history of psychiatric disorders and substance abuse were most likely to evidence MDD; these patients also had poorer overall social functioning than the nondepressed control group. In addition, patients with long-term depression showed greater impairment in psychosocial functioning and a greater disruption of daily activities than patients with short-term depression.

In a second study, McAllister and Ferrell (2002) uncovered a relationship between TBI and the development of schizophrenia-like symptoms such as mania and hallucinations. They reported that a meta-analytic review of a number of studies revealed a prevalence of 0.7% to 9.8%, thus showing that psychotic symptoms are more common among TBI patients, occuring 2 or 3 times greater than expected by chance. When taken cumulatively, the data indicate that patients with TBI show a higher incidence of psychiatric disorders such as MDD and other forms of psychosis than noninjured individuals. Researchers have suggested that studies of mood disorders and psychosis in TBI patients might provide insight into the pathogenesis of a range of other psychiatric illnesses (McAllister & Ferrell, 2002; Ricardo & Robinson, 2002).

References

Grof, P. (2002). Mood disorders—new definitions, treatment directions, and understanding. *Canadian Journal of Psychiatry*, *47(2)*, 123–124.

Joffe, R. T. (2003). Treating mood disorders. *Journal of Psychiatry & Neuroscience*, *28(3)*, 1.

MacAllister, T. W. & Ferrell, R. B. (2002). Evaluation and treatment of psychosis after traumatic brain injury. *NeuroRehabilitation*, *17*, 357–368.

Ricardo, J. & Robinson, R. G. (2002). Mood disorders following traumatic brain injury. *NeuroRehabilitation*, *17*, 311–324.

Thorpe, L., Whitney, D. K., Kutcher, S. P., & Kennedy, S. H. (2001). Clinical guidelines for the treatment of depressive disorders: Special populations. *Canadian Journal of Psychiatry*, *46* (Suppl. 1), 63–76.

Volkmar, F. R. (2002). Changing perspectives on mood disorders in children. *TheAmerican Journal of Psychiatry*, *159(6)*, 893–894.

Chapter 11, Schizophrenia and Other Psychotic Disorders

Of the myriad of psychiatric disorders, schizophrenia is one of the most frequently researched topics. A recent key word query of a national database produced over 3,900 hits for the topic of schizophrenia; at least 100 articles were published just from January to mid-March 2003. Much of the research has focused on etiology, diagnosis, treatment, and comorbidity of the disorder with other disorders. Schizophrenia and other psychotic disorders have a poor prognosis and little hope for positive outcomes (Spaniol, Wewiorski, Gagne, & Anthony, 2002). However, recent literature has focused on the recovery aspects of the disorder. According to Hoffmann and Kupper (2002), in a meta-analysis of twentieth-century literature focusing on the outcomes of schizophrenia, approximately 40% of patients afflicted with the disorder will show some improvement in the 6 years following diagnosis. These findings imply that with an effective treatment program, a sizable number of individuals could recover from schizophrenia. Because of varying conceptualizations of what constitutes a successful recovery from schizophrenia, the notion has remained elusive. However, Noordsy et al. (2002) have proposed an operational definition of schizophrenia that contains three parts: (a) hope, (b) taking responsibility for managing illness and wellness issues, and (c) getting on with life beyond the illness. Their goal in conceptualizing this definition was to outline a usable and testable framework from which recovery could be evaluated.

Loss of hope is prevalent among individuals with mental disorders. As they find themselves isolated, stigmatized, shunned, and misunderstood by society, individuals feel that they cannot effect change and are likely to lose motivation; thus they may subsequently stop putting forth the effort. Therefore, hope is a necessary antecedent to motivation, and motivation is a prerequisite for action (Noordsy et al., 2002). Taking personal responsibility involves three subcomponents. The first is acceptance of the presence of illness. The shift away from denial to acceptance might be the impetus that propels an individual toward recovery. This shift may lead individuals to develop a more realistic self-identity with respect to their illness and prospects of wellness. In turn, the attitude shift may enable individuals to develop a healthy life-style by taking steps that center on tasks, activities, and relationships that establish meaning and continuity in their lives. Taking responsibility for illness management includes obtaining proper treatment for the disorder. Successful treatment requires that patients participate in a therapeutic program in which they take medications as required and establish other routines, such as proper diet and adequate exercise, to further enhance their overall health and wellness.

To get on with life beyond the illness, patients must reintegrate themselves into society and become functioning, productive citizens. This phase has three sub-components. The first component centers on the individual's perception of his or her role in life. The therapist's objective is to help clients develop a self-identity that enables them to move away from viewing themselves as patients to focusing on other roles that they hold in society. "Identities such as parent, church member, reliable employee, voter, and student were critical components of self-identity beyond one's illness" (Noordsy et. al., 2002, p. 321). The second subcomponent of getting on with life is the establishment of meaningful interpersonal relationships. Because of the social disruptions caused by psychiatric disorders, sufferers of schizophrenia often find themselves without an interpersonal support system. According to Noordsy et al. (2002), clients frequently cite meaningful relationships, family relationships, and intimate relationships as being an important component of life. Because all members of society relate these types of relationships to self-definitions and personal satisfaction, it is understandable that such relationships also serve as crucial components of the recovery process. The third subcomponent of getting on with life centers on developing meaningful work or other structured activities. These actions tend to help the client remain focused on self-care and illness management. Individuals may achieve this goal by engaging in work activities, by serving as volunteers, and by participating in community organizations such as churches, clubs, or athletic groups. Noordsy et al., offered a definition of recovery that is "practical, measurable and accessible, bridging a range of potential stakeholders and applications" (p. 325).

To shed some light on the process of recovery in patients with schizophrenia, Spaniol et al., (2002) conducted a qualitative study of the psychosocial recovery of 242 patients with varying diagnoses of mental disorders, 12 of which were included in the study. The researchers conducted open-ended interviews two or three times a year to gain information about the patients' life experiences during the previous months. The participants provided descriptions of their experiences which clustered into three categories, or three phases of recovery; each phase was associated with specific tasks. Phase 1 was described as being overwhelmed by the disability. During this period individuals come to learn of the presence of a disorder, and while they may have a strong desire to affiliate with others, interpersonal relationships are either tentative or nonexistent. This phase can last anywhere from a few months to several years. The major task of this phase is establishing a context for understanding the disorder. Phase 2 of recovery is characterized by a patient's struggle with the existence of the disability. This phase is characterized by efforts to understand what is happening. An individual may recognize the need to cope with the disorder and the need to have a satisfying life; however, the individual may expend considerable energy and effort simply accepting the existence of the disorder. The major task of this phase is to gain some personal control of the illness in order to minimize the personal, social, and emotional difficulties that it causes. Achieving this goal often requires effective coping skills and access to professional services as well as strong financial and social support systems. Phase 3 of recovery involves efforts to live with the disorder. The major task of this phase is to gain some control of the illness and of oneself. In this phase the individual develops confidence and a stronger sense of control over self. In working through this phase, individuals may require the administration of psychotropic medication as a short-term measure; however, patients in this phase have realized the possibility of having a satisfying life. Eventually they develop adequate coping strategies and they also devise methods for engaging in meaningful roles and activities. Spaniol et al. (2002) also conceptualized a fourth phase of recovery, which is living beyond the disability. Although none of the patients in their study had reached this point, the researchers developed this theoretical basis from a review of previous literature. In the final phase, individuals feel connected to others, they are able to establish meaningful roles, and they also feel they have a purpose in life. In this phase, individuals progress to the point that the mental disorder becomes a part of their self-identity that does not interfere with their overall functioning and quality of life. As part of the study, Spaniol et al. (2002) also recognized three factors that posed challenges to recovery: comorbid substance abuse, environmental context, and age of onset of schizophrenia. Substance abuse presented an added dimension with which individuals struggled to cope. Dual treatment of substance abuse tended to draw on more professional and individual resources than did management of a single illness. Environmental factors such as poverty combined with race presented additional challenges. Patients who lived in poverty exerted a great deal of effort trying to obtain or sustain the minimal resources needed for survival. Members of minority groups faced the double stigma of minority status and mental illness. In both cases, members of poverty and minority groups faced additional challenges imposed by their environment context.

In another study, Russinova, Wewiorski, Lyass, Rogers, and Massaro (2002) investigated the correlates of vocational recovery and vocational success in 109 participants who were diagnosed with schizophrenia, schizoaffective disorder, and unspecified psychosis. The researchers developed a baseline survey organized into eight sections: current employment, satisfaction with current employment, past employment, everyday life, work and everyday life, challenges at work, psychiatric condition, and personal background. Results revealed that respondents were functioning well in the areas measured. Of the respondents, 93% were living independently and 88% were living in residences that did not have a connection to the mental health system. A large percentage of the respondents indicated that they had social contacts outside their household. During the preceding month, 92% of the respondents had communicated with a relative and 92% had contacted a friend who was not a roommate. Almost 54% of the respondents indicated that they had contact with both a relative and a friend outside the household. Concerning the vocational characteristics of the group, of the 71% of the subjects ($n = 77$) in the study who had worked prior to their illness, 91% ($n = 70$) indicated being employed for 1 year after the illness and 68% ($n = 60$) reported being on one job for more than a year. Slightly fewer than 50% ($n = 52$) reported that their work had been interrupted for longer than a year after the onset of the illness. Only 17% ($n = 18$) of the participants reported using vocational services to obtain their current positions. Regarding the number of hours worked per week, 60% ($n = 65$) of the respondents worked at least 35 hours per week and 84% ($n = 92$) worked at least 20 hours per week. The researchers concluded that the data offered substantial evidence that vocational recovery and vocational success are viable outcomes for individuals diagnosed with schizophrenia spectrum disorders.

Cumulatively, recent research on various aspects of recovery from the schizophrenic spectrum disorders offers promise and hope for the outcome of individuals diagnosed with schizophrenia. "Recovery has emerged as a crucial concept in the treatment of individuals with mental illness" (Noordsy et al., 2002). Current research reveals that recovery is a multidimensional construct involving various tasks, challenges, supports, and processes (Spaniol et al., 2002). Researchers have demonstrated that with the proper support and treatment, individuals with schizophrenia and related disorders can be restored to a full and productive life (Hoffman & Kupper 2002; Noordsy et al., 2002; Russinova et al., 2002).

References

Hoffman, H. & Kupper, Z. (2002). Facilitators of psychosocial recovery from schizophrenia. *International Review of Psychiatry, 14*, 293–302.

Noordsy, D., Torrey, W., Mueser, K., Mead, S., O'Keefe, C., & Lindy, F. (2002). Recovery from severe mental illness: An interpersonal and functional outcome definition. *International Review of Psychiatry, 14*, 318–326.

Russinova, A., Wewiorski, N. J., Lyass, A., Rogers, S. E., & Massaro, J. M. (2002). Correlates of vocational recovery for persons with schizophrenia. *International Review of Psychiatry, 14*, 303–311.

Spaniol, L., Wewiorski, N. J., Gagne, C., & Anthony, W. A. (2002). The process of recovery from schizophrenia. *International Review of Psychiatry, 14*, 327–336.

Chapter 14, Disorders of Childhood and Adolescence

Childhood mental disorders are broken into two categories, externalizing and internalizing disorders. However, use of these broad categories as a guide to reviewing research on disorders in childhood and adolescence may lead to limited findings. For instance, a recent key word search generated a list of only 26 studies that incorporated the phrase "externalizing disorders," and 22 hits were produced for "internalizing disorders." Conversely, a key word search for "attention-deficit/hyperactivity disorder" (ADHD) produced 1,495 hits in the same database. Therefore, it is more useful to investigate the subcategories of child and adolescent disorders than the broad categories when searching for publications.

Attention-Deficit/Hyperactivity Disorder (ADHD)

At least 270 studies were published on ADHD between January 2002 and March 2003. Much of that research focused on children with ADHD and extended previous findings; few articles addressed the longitudinal course of ADHD in adulthood. The symptoms of ADHD in adults are often reflective of those found in children and are associated with education, occupation, and interpersonal problems (Weiss & Murray, 2003).

Prevalence ADHD occurs in about 3% to 5% of children and 2% to 6% of adults (Fisher, 2002; Weiss & Murray, 2003). Although the prevalence of the disorder for males is greater than females (nearly 10 to 1, respectively) in childhood, the ratio drops 2 to 1 in adulthood (Elliott, 2002; Harvard Mental Health Letter, 2002; Stern, Garg, & Stern, 2002). The exact etiology of the disorder is unknown; however, there is a strong hereditary component. One in four children with ADHD will also have a sibling with the disorder. In addition, it is not uncommon for one or both parents of children being evaluated for ADHD to discover that they have ADHD as well. Estimates for the heritability component of ADHD run as high as 60% to 80% (Harvard Mental Health Letter, 2002). Although many youngsters outgrow the disorder, for some 30% to 50% the condition persists into adulthood (Elliott, 2002; Stern et al., 2002). ADHD is most likely to persist in the presence of other conditions such as a mood disorder or an extant family history of ADHD.

Diagnosis The first step in determining effective treatment strategies for adults with attention disorders is to obtain an accurate diagnosis, and doing so is no easy task. Although the DSM–IV provides criteria for differentiating among the three subcategories of attention-deficit disorders (hyperactive, inattentive, and combined hyperactive and inattentive), diagnosing ADHD in adulthood is by far the most difficult because a prerequisite for diagnosis of adult ADHD is the presence of ADHD symptoms in childhood (Elliott, 2002; Stern et al., 2002). According to Stern et al., one reason for the difficulty in diagnosing ADHD in adults is that the three components of inattention, impulsivity, and hyperactivity seen in children are often not found in adults. Inattention, found in 90% of adults with ADHD, is the component most frequently seen. As individuals mature, the rates of impulsivity and hyperactivity seem to decline (although they do not extinguish completely). Another factor that contributes to the difficulty of diagnosing adult ADHD is the requirement that such a diagnosis must exclude the presence of other conditions such as anxiety, mood, or personality disorders. However, several studies have shown that many adults with ADHD also have other disorders (Elliott, 2002; Stern et al., 2002). Often these disorders are interactive in nature. For instance, patients with ADHD may appear confused, anxious, depressed, and agitated. Similarly, anxious and depressed patients may appear inattentive, distracted, and disorganized. These interactive processes often make it difficult for clinicians to determine which of the comorbid conditions are pri-

mary causes of personal difficulties and which are symptoms or byproducts of the primary cause.

Implications The presence of ADHD in adults carries with it at least one major implication, the necessity to provide accommodations for those diagnosed with the disorder. Since the passage of Section 504 of the Rehabilitation Act in 1973 and the later passage of the Americans With Disabilities Act (ADA, 1990), ADHD and other learning disabilities (LDs) have been identified as a spectrum of disabilities for which individuals are entitled to accommodations (Gordon, Lewandwoski, Murphy, & Dempsy, 2002). The number of requests for accommodations from college-bound students has been increasing. Although the ADA makes provisions for accommodations to be made for students with disabilities such as LDs and ADHD, the law has resulted in frustration and confusion. Some clinicians and researchers have argued that there is a great deal of variability and flexibility in terms of how some professionals interpret the definitions and criteria of the ADA. Consequently, there is little consistency among various agencies, professionals, and educational institutions regarding the application of ADA guidelines for making accommodations for students diagnosed with LD and ADHD. Gordon et al. (2002) speculated that one reason for the disparities may be the extent of training received about the ADA. These researchers conducted a study to determine clinicians' knowledge of the ADA and diagnostic practices for assessing LD and ADHD.

The study consisted of a 21-item researcher-developed questionnaire that addressed clinicians' knowledge of diagnostic practices for LD, ADHD, and/or psychiatric disorders. A total of 14 participants completed the survey. The results were presented in three categories: (a) areas of general agreement, (b) areas of general disagreement, and (c) current training needs. As an area of agreement, clinicians endorsed the practice of ruling out other disorders before assigning a diagnosis of ADHD to a client, a practice that is consistent with making a differential diagnosis for the disorder. The greatest area of disagreement was the extent of impairment that is required to validate the existence of a disability as required by law. A second area of disagreement occurred regarding the age of onset of ADHD. According to Gordon et al. (2002), almost 41% of the respondents agreed with the statement "An adult can be classified as having ADHD even if he or she had no significant childhood impairment, never required accommodations prior to graduate school, and had no history of brain injury" (p. 360). This finding indicated that a large number of clinicians in this study disagreed with, or at least deviated from, the criteria for ADHD as specified in the DSM–IV. Concerning the need for training, the majority of respondents indicated a lack of formal training in ADA law. Most, 77%, indicated that they had educated themselves about the topic. In addition, 83% indicated a desire for additional training on the law and its implications for their work. The findings of the study reflect the complexity of issues surrounding the diagnosis of ADHD in adults.

Treatment and outcomes   The first step in effective treatment involves an accurate diagnosis of ADHD in adults. Because of the comorbidity of ADHD and other disorders, medical treatments are the most frequently used form of intervention (Stern et al., 2002). Although medications provide short-term relief from symptoms associated with ADHD, they have not been shown to produce any long-term effects. Similarly, psychosocial interventions have been demonstrated to provide short-term benefits, but no long-term gains (Stern et al., 2002; Weiss & Murray, 2003). Therefore, there are three possible outcomes for adults with ADHD. A percentage of individuals will function as effectively as adults without ADHD (about 30%); most will continue to have sustained personal, interpersonal, and occupational difficulties; and a small percentage (10% to 15%) will manifest other psychiatric or antisocial disorders.

Oppositional Defiant Disorder (ODD) and Conduct Disorder (CD)

Although the outcome of ADHD is particularly troubling to the individual, the outcome of the other two externalizing disorders has much wider consequences. In addition to the personal and family turmoil precipitated by ODD and CD, these disorders, when left untreated, have sociological implications. ODD in childhood is a developmental characteristic which precedes CD in adolescence, and CD in adolescents is linked to development of antisocial personality disorder (APD) in adults. A sizable number of individuals diagnosed with these childhood disorders progress to antisocial behaviors in adulthood. About 50% of adults with APD evidenced some degree of antisocial behavior in childhood or adolescence (Simons, Chao, Conger, & Elder, 2001; Loeber et al., 2002). Failure to adequately treat these disorders results in untold societal suffering due to the nature of the antisocial behaviors and the cost of addressing their consequences (Shamsie, 2001).

ODD   According to Simons et al. (2001), there are two prevailing theoretical perspectives as to what causes ODD in children. The first perspective is the latent-trait model, which proposes that such behaviors result from an interaction between adverse family dynamics, a difficult temperament, and neuropsychological deficits within the individual. Hence from this perspective, the antisocial behavior is seen as an individual trait that is mediated by the environment, and parenting practices are believed to be most influential in the early years. The latent-trait perspective posits that by the time a child with ODD reaches adolescence, the trait that drives antisocial behavior becomes ingrained, and thus parenting is likely to have little effect on changing it. The second perspective views antisocial behavior as being a result of adverse social influences, chief among them the parent-child dynamic. The "social influence perspective asserts that parents of difficult children often engage in little monitoring or discipline and that this low parental involvement increases the child's opportunity to experiment with delinquent behavior" (Simons, et al., p. 65). Hence, ODD becomes a byproduct of inept parenting skills exerted during adolescence.

Simons et al. (2001) investigated the merits of each of these perspectives in explaining the stability of antisocial behavior in youth, using data from the Iowa Youth and Families Project (IYFP) in a longitudinal study of two-parent families and their children. The data was colleted over a period of 4 years using the same collection procedures. Data regarding ODD were collected through observational and parental reports. The observation measures consisted of ratings of the frequency of antisocial behavior toward other family members, as documented on videotaped tasks. Both mothers and fathers completed the Revised Behavior Problem Checklist. Measures of parenting practices were documented through observer ratings, parent self-reports, and child reports. Both parents completed a 13-item questionnaire that asked about parenting practices in the areas of monitoring, discipline, consistency of discipline, and inductive reasoning. The observers also rated the parents along the previous dimensions as well as the added dimensions of hostility, communication, coerciveness, and warmth. The adolescents used the same questionnaires to rate each parent on the first four dimensions. The adolescents were also administered self-report instruments that addressed their affiliation with deviant peers and measured the nature and frequency of their delinquent behaviors. The study presented the following findings.

1. ODD was strongly related to ineffective parenting. In addition, ineffective parenting in late childhood predicted increases in affiliation with deviant peers and delinquency in adolescence.
2. ODD was negatively related to changes in parenting practices during adolescence. The parents in this study demonstrated little parental involvement in late childhood and then switched to more controlling behavior in adolescence. The researchers posit that this change may have been precipitated by the

increase in antisocial behavior exhibited in adolescence.

3. Reduced parental control was related to increased affiliation with deviant peers, but it was not related to increased delinquent behavior.

4. At the end of the study, parents of children with ODD continued to exert less control than parents of other children.

The researchers concluded that the data supported both the latent-trait perspective and the social influence perspective. Apparently some children may be predisposed to engage in antisocial behavior, but environmental factors also moderate that behavior. Low parental control appears to be one of those factors, and involvement with deviant peers may be another.

CD CD is the most common reason for child psychiatric referrals; such referrals involve 30% to 50% of all cases (Bassarath, 2001). Like ODD, CD is positively correlated with acts of delinquency. Although no single factor serves as an accurate predictor of future delinquent behaviors, according to Bassarath, characteristics such as past offenses, deviant peers, poor social relations, substance abuse, and antisocial parents strongly predict future delinquency. In addition, early aggression, low family economic status, psychological characteristics, parent-child relationships, school attitude and performance, and medical or physical conditions serve as moderate predictors. Mild predictors are factors such as family size, broken home, abusive parenting, and family stress. Although CD or delinquency cannot be accurately predicted from a single variable, the coexistence of multiple risk factors (the presence of 4 or 5 factors) increases risk by 31%. Because of the monetary and social costs associated with CD, it is imperative to identify effective intervention and treatment programs. Such programs begin by providing support to families of children with CD.

According to Wood (2002), parents of children with CD frequently feel that they are blamed for their children's behavior. These parents need help to manage the conflict they endure and to improve communication with their adolescents. Because ODD and CD are difficult to treat, the best strategy is to prevent their occurrence. According to Markward and Bride (2001), therapeutic practices are guided by the belief that changing the behavior of one member of a family will ultimately influence a change in other members as well. Effective family-centered practices are guided by the following principles.

1. The home is the best place to help families; hence, effective intervention strategies require the observation of families in their homes. Such observations may reveal problematic interactions and provide the opportunity for immediate feedback on how to correct those dynamics.

2. Families learn the skills they need to solve their own problems.

3. Intervention strategies are individualized and are based on the particular needs of the family.

4. Intervention strategies are responsive to a family's immediate needs and tuned to the family's long-term goals.

5. The family is seen as a system in which the behavior of the various members influences the behavior of other members.

6. A collaborative relationship exists between the family and the practitioner.

7. Family-centered practices promote distributive social justice.

The findings of Simons et al. (2001) underscore the importance of research on family-centered interventions as a means of minimizing the long-term effects of externalizing disorders such as ODD and CD.

Frick (2001) further identified four effective treatment strategies for CD: contingency management, parent management training, cognitive-behavioral skills training (CBST), and stimulant medication. Contingency management is a structured approach to managing the behavior of adolescents with CD. The basic components of the program involve establishing goals, implementing a system to monitor achievement of those goals, providing a system of reinforcement for obtaining goals, and establishing consequences for inappropriate behavior. Such programs have been demonstrated to be effective in a range of settings. Parent management training focuses on developing skills that will assist parents in improving communication with their children, changing their children's inappropriate behaviors, effectively monitoring their children's activities, and developing effective discipline strategies. CBST programs focus on improving the deficits in social cognition and social-problem-solving that are associated with CD. Stimulant medication was most effective when used to treat those individuals who were also diagnosed with ADHD. The efficacy of this treatment strategy may be due to the fact that 60% to 90% of the patients referred for CD also have ADHD.

It must be cautioned that no single method of treatment has been shown to completely suppress the problems associated with externalizing behaviors. Rather, the various treatment approaches have reduced the number of manifested problem behaviors. Because of their complex etiology and diagnosis, research is still needed to find the best prevention, intervention, and treatment strategies for the externalizing disorders.

References

Bassarath, L. (2001). Conduct disorder: Biopsychosocial review. *Canadian Journal of Psychiatry, 46(7)*, 609–616.

Eliott, H. (2002). Attention deficit disorder in adults: A guide for the primary care physician. *Southern Medical Journal, 95(7)*, 736–742.

Frick P.J. (2001). Effective interventions for children and adolescents with conduct disorder. *Canadian Journal of Psychiatry, 46(7)*, 597–608.

Fisher, A. (2002). I realized I have ADHD, and now I want my job back. *Fortune, 146(6)*, 208.

Gordon, M., Lewandwoski, L., Murphy, K., & Dempsy, K. (2002). ADA-based accommodations in higher education: A survey of clinicians about documentation requirements and diagnostic standards. *Journal of Learning Disabilities, 35(4)*, 173–186.

Harvard Mental Health Letter (2002, November). Attention deficit disorder in adults. *19(6)*, 3–6.

Loreber, R., Burke, J.D., & Lahey, B. F. (2002). What are adolescent antecedents to antisocial personality disorder? *Criminal Behaviour and Mental Health, 12*, 24–36.

Markward, M. J., & Bride, B. (2001). Oppositional defiant disorder and the need for family-centered practice in schools. *Children & Schools, 23(2)*, 73–83.

Shamsie, J. (2001). Conduct disorder: A challenge to child psychiatry. *Canadian Journal of Medicine, 46(7)*, 593–594.

Simons, R. L., Chao, W., Conger, R. D., & Elder, G. H. (2001). Quality of parenting as a mediator of the effect of childhood defiance on adolescent friendship choices and delinquency: A growth curve analysis. *Journal of Marriage & Family, 63(1)*, 63–79.

Stern, H. P., Garg, A., & Stern, T. P. (2002). When children with attention-deficit/hyperactivity disorder become adults. *Southern Medical Journal, 95(9)*, 985–991.

Weiss, M. & Murray, C. (2002). Assessment and management of attention-deficit/hyperactivity disorder in adults. *Canadian Medical Association Journal, 168(6)*, 715–722.

Wood, C. (2002) Supporting the parents of adolescents with conduct disorder. *Paediatric Nursing, 14(8)*, 24–26.

Chapter 15, Pervasive Developmental Disorders

Much recent research on the topic of pervasive developmental disorders has centered on autism. In fact, a key word search in a national database for the phrase "autistic disorder" produced 387 hits for the period covering January 2002 to February 2003. A key word search of the phrase "pervasive developmental disorders" produced only 8 hits for the same period. A large part of the research on autism has centered on attempting to distinguish autism from other developmental disorders such as Asperger's syndrome, Rett's disorder, atypical autism, and childhood disintegrative disorder. After reviewing the classification criteria for pervasive developmental disorder as set forth in the DSM–IV and as specified in the International Classification of Diseases, 10th edition, (World Health Organization, 1993), Szatmari (as cited in Freeman, Cronin, & Candela, 2002) concluded that there was not enough evidence to support dividing the various disorders into separate categories. He also concluded that there was a problem in the conceptualization of the various developmental disorders. Because these disorders share the same characteristics and differ only in terms of the age of onset and individual history, the term "autism spectrum disorders"(ASDs) is currently being used to refer to the disorders (Szatmari, 2003).

Prevalence Recent studies have focused on determining whether the incidence of autism has increased in the past 2 years. According to Gottlieb (2003), a study conducted by the Centers for Disease Control (CDC) in Atlanta found that the number of cases of autism in a five-county region was 10 times greater than reported in the 1980s. The CDC study found that for every 1,000 children aged 3 to 10 years, there were 3.4 cases of mild to severe autism. Surveys for the 1980s reported only 4 to 5 cases for every 10,000 children. The study found that males were four times more likely to be affected than females. If the criteria were expanded to include all cases of autism, the rate could reach as high as 63 cases per 10,000 children (Szatmari, 2003). Although the prevalence of ASDs is higher than previously reported, the reason for the rising number is not clear. Gottlieb proposed that the increase could be due to the expanded definition of autism; it could be due to greater awareness of the disorder; or it could be due to greater accuracy in terms of assessment and diagnosis of the disorder.

Etiology The extensive amount of recent literature on autism has led to several conceptual changes regarding its causes. First, it is now understood that genetics play a large role in the transmission of the disorder. Second, environmental factors also play a role. According to Szatmari (2003), preliminary evidence supports the hypothesis that thalidomide and anticonvulsants taken during pregnancy can cause ASDs. In previous years there had been much publicity regarding a possible link between the measles, mumps, and rubella (MMR) vaccine and the onset of autism. However, a large body of recent research contraindicates such a link.

After investigating the records of 500,000 children born in Denmark between 1991 and 1998, Madsen et al. (2002) failed to find a link between the MMR vaccine and autism. Included in the study were both children who received the MMR vaccine and those who did not. The study failed to find a difference in the prevalence of ASDs among vaccinated and unvaccinated children. According to the study, the MMR vaccine was introduced in Denmark in 1987, and the increase in autism did not begin until the mid–1990s. The researchers concluded that there is no connection between autism and the MMR vaccine. A second study conducted by Taylor et al. (2002) in five communities near London, England, produced similar results. This study investigated the hypothesis that a new variant of autism, including not only developmental regression, but also bowel problems, was associated with MMR vaccine. The study compared frequency of these atypical symptoms in children born in the 10 years before the vaccine was introduced and the 10 years after its use began. The researchers found no difference in the frequency of symptoms in the two groups of children and concluded that the vaccine use was not related either to autism or to the hypothesized variant form.

Long-term familial consequences Autism and related disorders have a severe and devastating effect on the individual. The effects on family members are equally devastating. Gray (2002) reported findings of a 10-year longitudinal study of the social experiences of children with autism and their families. The study included 24 children diagnosed with autism as defined in the DSM–IIIR and 35 of their parents. The children ranged in age from 4 to 19 years. The study documented both negative and positive outcomes. With regard to negative outcomes, the parents reported very high levels of emotional distress and psychological distress in the early years after initial diagnosis. The parents also reported career problems, with mothers reporting the most severe problems. The parents also expressed concern about their other children and how the presence of a child with autism would affect them. Quite often families with autistic children face a great deal of frustration as they attempt to socialize with others. Because of a general lack of societal knowledge and understanding of the disorder, many families often face rejection and isolation. Further, the parents expressed anxiety as they contemplated their children's future. Most of the parents had initially hoped their children would eventually improve enough so that they could live on their own; however, as time progressed, those hopes declined, and the parents

faced anxiety over finding residential placement for their offspring with autism. One of the most distressing issues for the parents was coping with violence from adolescent or adult offspring with autism

On a positive note, the families in the study found effective ways of coping with the stress induced by their children's disorder. Many reported growing closer to their extended families, and several reported success in finding friends who accepted their child's condition. In spite of the lack of adequate residential facilities, especially for violent children, overall, the study found that the majority of parents concluded that their situation was better than it had been in the previous 10 years.

Although there is still much to be learned regarding the pervasive developmental disorders, one point is clear: appropriate diagnosis is absolutely essential to proper treatment. According to Freeman, Cronin, and Candela (2002), a comprehensive assessment includes taking a developmental history to obtain information about communication skills and early social interactions, use of rating scales as screening instruments for various developmental disorders, medical assessment to rule out the presence of treatable conditions, psychological assessment to allow for a diagnosis of the degree of disability, communication to assess the presence of disturbances in thought process or content, language assessment to determine the status of language processes, occupational and physical therapy assessment to determine the presence of motor difficulties or hypersensitivities, family assessment to evaluate the extant support system, mental status assessment, assessment of social interaction, and other assessments as necessary. Although this range of assessment may seem extensive, it is a vital part of making an accurate diagnosis and subsequently structuring an appropriate treatment strategy.

References

Freeman, B. J., Cronin, P., & Candela, P. (2002). Asperger syndrome or autistic disorder? *Focus on Autism & Other Developmental Disabilities, 17(3),* 145–151.

Gottlieb, S. (2003). U.S. study shows 10-fold increase in autism over the past 20 years. *British Medical Journal, 326(7380),* 71.

Gray, D. E. (2002). Ten years on: A longitudinal study of families of children with autism. *Journal of Intellectual & Developmental Disability, 27(3),* 215–222.

Madsen, K.M., Hviid, A., Vestergaard, M., Schendel, et al. (2002). A population-based study of measles, mumps, and rubella vaccination and autism. *New*

England Journal of Medicine, 347(19), 1477–1482.

Taylor, B., Miller, E., Lingam, R., Andrew, N., Simmons, A., & Stowe, J. (2002). Measles, mumps, rubella vaccination and bowel problems or develop mental regression in children with autism.

Population study. *British Medical Journal, 324(7334),* 393–396.

Szatmari, P. (2003). The causes of autism spectrum disorders. *British Medical Journal, 326(7382),* 172–173.

SINGLE PC LICENSE AGREEMENT AND LIMITED WARRANTY

READ THIS LICENSE CAREFULLY BEFORE OPENING THIS PACKAGE. BY OPENING THIS PACKAGE, YOU ARE AGREEING TO THE TERMS AND CONDITIONS OF THIS LICENSE. IF YOU DO NOT AGREE, DO NOT OPEN THE PACKAGE. PROMPTLY RETURN THE UNOPENED PACKAGE AND ALL ACCOMPANYING ITEMS TO THE PLACE YOU OBTAINED THEM [[FOR A FULL REFUND OF ANY SUMS YOU HAVE PAID FOR THE SOFTWARE]]. *THESE TERMS APPLY TO ALL LICENSED SOFTWARE ON THE DISK EXCEPT THAT THE TERMS FOR USE OF ANY SHAREWARE OR FREEWARE ON THE DISKETTES ARE AS SET FORTH IN THE ELECTRONIC LICENSE LOCATED ON THE DISK:*

1.   GRANT OF LICENSE and OWNERSHIP: The enclosed computer programs <<and data>> ("Software") are licensed, not sold, to you by Pearson Education, Inc. publishing as Prentice Hall ("We" or the "Company") and in consideration [[of your payment of the license fee, which is part of the price you paid]] [[of your purchase or adoption of the accompanying Company textbooks and/or other materials,]] and your agreement to these terms. We reserve any rights not granted to you. You own only the disk(s) but we and/or our licensors own the Software itself. This license allows you to use and display your copy of the Software on a single computer (i.e., with a single CPU) at a single location for <u>academic</u> use only, so long as you comply with the terms of this Agreement. You may make one copy for back up, or transfer your copy to another CPU, provided that the Software is usable on only one computer.

2.   RESTRICTIONS: You may <u>not</u> transfer or distribute the Software or documentation to anyone else. Except for backup, you may <u>not</u> copy the documentation or the Software. You may <u>not</u> network the Software or otherwise use it on more than one computer or computer terminal at the same time. You may <u>not</u> reverse engineer, disassemble, decompile, modify, adapt, translate, or create derivative works based on the Software or the Documentation. You may be held legally responsible for any copying or copyright infringement that is caused by your failure to abide by the terms of hese restrictions.

3.   TERMINATION: This license is effective until terminated. This license will terminate automatically without notice from the Company if you fail to comply with any provisions or limitations of this license. Upon termination, you shall destroy the Documentation and all copies of the Software. All provisions of this Agreement as to limitation and disclaimer of warranties, limitation of liability, remedies or damages, and our ownership rights shall survive termination.

4.   LIMITED WARRANTY AND DISCLAIMER OF WARRANTY: Company warrants that for a period of 60 days from the date you purchase this SOFTWARE (or purchase or adopt the accompanying textbook), the Software, when properly installed and used in accordance with the Documentation, will operate in substantial conformity with the description of the Software set forth in the Documentation, and that for a period of 30 days the disk(s) on which the Software is delivered shall be free from defects in materials and workmanship under normal use. The Company does <u>not</u> warrant that the Software will meet your requirements or that the operation of the Software will be uninterrupted or error-free. Your only remedy and the Company's only obligation under these limited warranties is, at the Company's option, return of the disk for a refund of any amounts paid for it by you or replacement of the disk. THIS LIMITED WARRANTY IS THE ONLY WARRANTY PROVIDED BY THE COMPANY AND ITS LICENSORS, AND THE COMPANY AND ITS LICENSORS DISCLAIM ALL OTHER WARRANTIES, EXPRESS OR IMPLIED, INCLUDING WITHOUT LIMITATION, THE IMPLIED WARRANTIES OF MERCHANTABILITY AND FITNESS FOR A PARTICULAR PURPOSE. THE COMPANY DOES NOT WARRANT, GUARANTEE OR MAKE ANY REPRESENTATION REGARDING THE ACCURACY, RELIABILITY, CURRENTNESS, USE, OR RESULTS OF USE, OF THE SOFTWARE.

5.   LIMITATION OF REMEDIES AND DAMAGES: IN NO EVENT, SHALL THE COMPANY OR ITS EMPLOYEES, AGENTS, LICENSORS, OR CONTRACTORS BE LIABLE FOR ANY INCIDENTAL, INDIRECT, SPECIAL, OR CONSEQUENTIAL DAMAGES ARISING OUT OF OR IN CONNECTION WITH THIS LICENSE OR THE SOFTWARE, INCLUDING FOR LOSS OF USE, LOSS OF DATA, LOSS OF INCOME OR PROFIT, OR OTHER LOSSES, SUSTAINED AS A RESULT OF INJURY TO ANY PERSON, OR LOSS OF OR DAMAGE TO PROPERTY, OR CLAIMS OF THIRD PARTIES, EVEN IF THE COMPANY OR AN AUTHORIZED REPRESENTATIVE OF THE COMPANY HAS BEEN ADVISED OF THE POSSIBILITY OF SUCH DAMAGES. IN NO EVENT SHALL THE LIABILITY OF THE COMPANY FOR DAMAGES WITH RESPECT TO THE SOFTWARE EXCEED THE AMOUNTS ACTUALLY PAID BY YOU, IF ANY, FOR THE SOFTWARE OR THE ACCOMPANYING TEXTBOOK. BECAUSE SOME JURISDICTIONS DO NOT ALLOW THE LIMITATION OF LIABILITY IN CERTAIN CIRCUMSTANCES, THE ABOVE LIMITATIONS MAY NOT ALWAYS APPLY TO YOU.